N is for Nature

A Watercolor Alphabet Adventure Through Nature

Written by Missy Patterson

Copyright © [2025] by Missy Patterson.
All rights reserved.

For Maverick,
may you always see the magic in nature

A is for Acorn

B is for Butterfly

C is for Coral

D is for Desert

E is for Eagle

F is for Frog

G is for Glacier

H is for Honeybee

I is for Island

J is for Jellyfish

K is for Kapok tree

L is for Lightning

M is for Mountain

N is for Narwhal

O is for Oyster

P is for Peach tree

Q is for Quail

R is for River

S is for Snow leopard

T is for Tidal wave

U is for Universe

V is for Volcano

W is for Willow tree

X is for Xerophyte

Y is for Yellowfin fish

Z is for Zebra

Glossary

An acorn is the tiny seed of a giant oak tree. It's a small, hard, oval-shaped nut with a little rough cap on top, and you usually see them dropping to the ground in the fall. An acorn is super important because it contains everything needed to grow a massive oak tree someday, and lots of forest animals, like squirrels and deer, love to eat them as a yummy, healthy snack!

A butterfly is a beautiful insect with large, brightly colored wings that allow it to flutter from flower to flower. Every butterfly starts its life as a crawling caterpillar, then hides inside a protective shell called a chrysalis, and finally emerges with wings in a process called metamorphosis. They use their long, straw-like tongue to sip sweet nectar from flowers, which helps them survive and helps plants make new seeds.

Coral looks like rock or a strange underwater plant, but it is actually a community of tiny living animals called polyps that build hard, stony skeletons around themselves. Millions of these polyps grow together to create huge underwater structures called coral reefs, which are like the bustling, colorful cities of the ocean, providing food and shelter for over one-quarter of all sea life.

A desert is a huge, dry place where very little rain falls, making it difficult for plants and animals to live. Even though they are dry, deserts can be either very hot during the day (like the Sahara) or very cold (like the Gobi), but all of them are home to amazing, tough creatures, like camels and cacti.

An eagle is a large, powerful bird of prey famous for its amazing eyesight and incredible flying skills. It has a big, hooked beak and sharp claws called talons that it uses to catch and carry fish, rabbits, and other small animals. Eagles build their giant nests, called aeries, high up on cliffs or in tall trees and are often seen as a symbol of strength and freedom.

A frog is an amazing jumping animal that can live both on land and in water, which is why it is called an amphibian. All frogs hatch from eggs laid in the water as little swimming creatures called tadpoles, and they slowly grow legs and lose their tails to become adult frogs. They have bulging eyes, smooth skin, and a super long, sticky tongue they use to snatch insects right out of the air.

A glacier is a huge, slow-moving river of ice that is so thick and heavy it can actually shape the land. Glaciers form in places where snow piles up year after year and never melts, getting squeezed tightly until it turns into solid ice. As they slide downhill very slowly, they pick up rocks and dirt, carving out valleys and mountainsides like a giant bulldozer.

A honeybee is a busy, buzzing insect that lives in a huge group called a colony, or hive, and works hard to make sweet, sticky honey from flower nectar. Honeybees are super important because as they fly from flower to flower collecting nectar, they also carry pollen, which helps plants make new seeds and fruits, including many of the foods we love to eat.

An island is any piece of land that is completely surrounded by water but is not big enough to be called a continent. Islands can form in different ways, such as when a volcano erupts from the ocean floor or when a piece of land breaks off from a larger continent, and they often have unique plants and animals that can't be found anywhere else.

A jellyfish is a beautiful sea creature that has no brain, no bones, and no heart, and is mostly made up of water, which makes it look like a clear, floating bell. It has long, stinging parts called tentacles that hang down and help it catch food, and it drifts through the ocean by opening and closing its bell-shaped body.

The kapok tree is one of the tallest trees found in the rainforest, often called the "King of the Forest," and its trunk is covered in giant spikes to protect itself. It is famous for growing huge seed pods that burst open to release a fluffy, light fiber, also called kapok, which floats on the wind like cotton and has been used for centuries to fill pillows and life jackets.

Lightning is a giant, sudden burst of electrical energy that appears as a bright, flashing streak in the sky during a thunderstorm. It happens when powerful electrical charges build up in the clouds and then rapidly jump to the ground or another cloud to balance the energy, causing the super-hot flash of light we see, which is quickly followed by the sound of thunder.

A mountain is a massive, tall section of Earth's surface that rises sharply, usually to a peak or summit, making it much higher than a hill. Mountains are formed when giant pieces of the Earth's crust slowly smash into each other, pushing the land upward, and they can have different climates at different heights, often having snow and ice near the very top.

A narwhal is a special type of whale that lives in the cold Arctic waters and is often called the "unicorn of the sea" because the male has a long, straight, spiraled tusk growing right out of its head. This tusk is actually a tooth up to 10 feet long, and scientists believe the narwhal uses it to fight, find food, and sense what's around it in the dark ocean.

An oyster is a soft sea creature that lives inside a hard, hinged shell and spends its entire adult life fixed to the bottom of the ocean or a reef. Oysters are well known for being able to create a beautiful, shiny pearl when a piece of sand or something else gets inside their shell and irritates them, so they cover it with a smooth layer to protect themselves.

A peach tree is a type of small tree that grows delicious, round, and fuzzy fruit called peaches. The tree blooms in the spring with beautiful pink flowers, and by summer, these flowers turn into the sweet, juicy fruit, which has a large, hard pit (or seed) right in the middle that you can plant to grow a new peach tree.

A quail is a small, plump bird that lives on the ground and is often recognized by a cute little plume or feather sticking up from the top of its head. Quails usually don't fly very high or far, but when they are scared, they can burst up into the air and fly away very quickly, and they like to live together in small groups called coveys.

A river is a large, natural stream of water that flows across the land, usually starting high up in mountains or hills and flowing downhill until it empties into a lake, a larger river, or the ocean. Rivers are incredibly important because they provide water for plants and animals, create rich soil along their banks, and act as natural highways for boats and fish.

A snow leopard is a beautiful, powerful wild cat that lives in the high, cold, and rocky mountains of Central Asia. Its thick, soft, spotted fur and long, bushy tail help it stay warm and blend into the snowy environment, and it is a very shy animal that uses its amazing strength to hunt goats and other large prey on the steep mountain slopes.

A tidal wave is an older name people sometimes use for a tsunami, which is a series of extremely powerful and large ocean waves caused by a sudden event like an earthquake or a volcanic eruption under the sea. A tsunami can travel across the ocean at great speeds, building up into a huge wall of water when it finally reaches shallow coastlines.

The Universe is absolutely everything that exists: all of space, all of time, and all of matter and energy, which includes Earth, the sun, all the stars, all the planets, and all the galaxies. It is so unbelievably huge that we can only see a tiny part of it, and scientists believe it is always growing bigger and bigger.

A volcano is a vent or opening in the Earth's crust that allows hot, melted rock, ash, and gases to escape from deep inside the Earth. When a volcano erupts, it is an incredible display of nature's power as hot magma (melted rock) pushes out, and once it is outside, it is called lava, which slowly cools down to form new land and mountains.

A willow tree is a flexible tree famous for its long, thin, drooping branches that seem to weep or hang down all the way to the ground, which is why it is often called a weeping willow. These trees grow very fast and love to be near water, like rivers and ponds, and their strong, flexible branches have been used for centuries to make baskets and furniture.

A xerophyte is a special kind of plant that is an expert at living in extremely dry places, like deserts. These plants have amazing tricks to survive with almost no water, such as having very thick, waxy skin to keep water inside, or growing long roots to find water deep in the ground, or even storing water in their stems and leaves, just like a cactus.

A yellowfin fish is a large type of tuna that swims very fast in the warm waters of the ocean and is easily recognized by its very long, bright yellow fins. These powerful fish are expert hunters

A zebra is a wild animal from Africa that looks like a horse but has a unique pattern of bold black and white stripes covering its entire body. Scientists believe these stripes confuse the animals' predators and biting insects, and just like a human's fingerprint, no two zebras have the exact same stripe pattern.

www.ingramcontent.com/pod-product-compliance
Lightning Source LLC
Chambersburg PA
CBHW061158030426

42337CB00003B/47